Act of God
Active God

Recovering from Natural Disasters

Dr. Gary Harbaugh

Fortress Press
Minneapolis

Cover design by Marti Naughton
Book design by Zan Ceeley

Library of Congress Cataloging-in-Publication Data
Harbaugh, Gary L.
    Act of God/active God : recovering from natural disasters / Gary L.
    Harbaugh.
        p. cm.
    Includes bibliographical references.
    ISBN 0-8006-3215-X (alk. paper)
    1. Disasters—Religious aspects—Christianity. I. Title.
BT161 .H37 2001
248.8'6—dc21
                                                    00-054352

Manufactured in the U.S.A.   AF 1–3215
05   04   03   02   01   1   2   3   4   5   6   7   8   9   10

To the Rev. Dr. Leon Phillips,
who before his retirement was the
first Director of Lutheran Disaster Response,
with deep respect
and appreciation for his mentoring,
his pastoral collegiality, his friendship,
and his willingness to give so much
to so many in times of disaster,
in the name of Christ.

Contents

You who live in the shelter of the Most High,
who abide in the shadow of the Almighty,
will say to the Lord, "My refuge and my fortress;
my God, in whom I trust."

Psalm 91:1-2

I am continually with you;
you hold my right hand.

Psalm 73:23

Let your heart take courage.

Psalm 27:14

Foreword

"Can atheists get insurance for acts of God?" As I read this "imponderable" recently in a newspaper's religion page, I was reminded there has been a lot of confusion over the years because of that little phrase, "act of God." Even Merriam-Webster's dictionary indicates the phrase was used as early as 1859 to describe "an extraordinary interruption by a natural cause (as a flood or earthquake) of the usual course of events that experience, prescience, or care cannot reasonably foresee or prevent."

There is a sharp contradiction between belief in a loving, benevolent God and a God who would willingly inflict destruction and death on the very people God created and redeemed. Disasters as "acts of God" confuse people affected by a disaster as well as those responding to help.

The church has always responded in times of disasters. From the very beginning, God's people have been responding in times of famines and floods, earthquakes and windstorms, fires and droughts. Why the church responds became clear as I was serving my second congregation. "Pastor, you couldn't pay me to do what I've done today," a council member, told me as we ended a day of shoveling smelly river water and mud from a basement in Wilkes-Barre, Pennsylvania. It was 1972, and Hurricane Agnes had caused massive flooding in the area. As I pondered his comment, I found a reason why the church is committed to disaster response ministry in the third chapter of St. Matthew: "Then Jesus came from Galilee to John at the Jordan, to be baptized. . . . when Jesus had been baptized, just as he came up from the water, suddenly the heavens were opened to him and he saw the Spirit of God descending like a dove and alighting on him. And a voice from heaven said, 'This is my Son, the Beloved, with whom I am well pleased.'" (Matt. 3:13-17). Jesus' baptism and the gift of the Spirit identify his mission to do God's work. It means the same for us. In our baptism we are also identified as God's beloved children, and we become part of the church family God creates by the Holy Spirit. Baptism gives us a mission to continue Jesus' ministry. We are Jesus' presence in today's world. How do we express our baptismal faith? To be spirit-filled, baptized Christians is to have a deep, loving concern for the lives of others in trouble and in misery. Each year those include the thousands whose lives are affected by the crises of disasters.

Whether the church is responding locally to a member whose house has burned—or is sending a team of volunteers to help in a nationally coordinated response to an impacted community in another part of the country—the confusion about a disaster as an "act of God" remains for both the helper and the survivor.

In this book, Dr. Gary Harbaugh provides insights and understandings to help persons of faith struggle with that seeming contradiction. Following examples of people who have experienced a variety of disasters, he confronts the faith issues from a profound theological perspective. Instead of seeing disasters as "acts of God," he shows that when disasters occur, God in fact is active: active in and through our questions, confusion, and doubts; active in and through our responses and actions; active in and through the community; and active in and through people of faith. He offers seven ways people of faith can transform disasters into times of blessings, and he provides helpful spiritual and biblical resources to strengthen Christians in times of disaster.

Gary Harbaugh has provided blessings to many over the course of his ministry, as a pastor, seminary professor, and writer. In times of disasters he serves as a Lutheran Disaster Response resource. Over the years he has offered Care for the Caregiver ministry to pastors, counselors, and staff impacted by disasters and involved in the church's response to disasters. He is a valued colleague and a trusted friend. His thoughtful and caring ministry has blessed many people. I trust this book will be a blessing for you and for all who, in times of disasters, are people of an "active God."

—GILBERT B. FURST
Director, Lutheran Disaster Response

1

Act of God

TORNADO!

Suddenly the sirens sounded! A long, ominous wail! It was very early in the morning, still dark outside. Mary had gone to sleep earlier, not quite recovered from the flu and feeling tired. John stayed up to read; he went to bed close to midnight. As he dropped off to sleep, the night was quiet, except for some distant thunder.

John was startled awake. Lightning was flashing and the thunder, no longer distant, was rattling the windows. John sensed there was something different about this storm. He turned on the TV, keeping the volume down so as not to awaken Mary. He was not surprised to see a weather bulletin streaming across the bottom of the screen. A tornado watch, which John had not known about before he went to bed, had turned into a tornado warning, and the weather forecaster announced the track of the fast-moving storm. The tornado was only minutes away, already on the ground, and heading directly toward where John and Mary lived!

What to do? John looked at Mary, who was still sleeping and unaware of the dangerous storm. John called quietly but urgently, "Mary! Mary!" Not quite fully awake, Mary's fatigue became mixed with alarm when she, too, saw the weather bulletin. The storm was becoming ever stronger and moving faster. When the sirens sounded, Mary cried out and ran to the bathroom, the most protected room in the house, calling back over her shoulder for John to follow her.

John lingered a few moments, looking out the window. The lightning flashes were so bright and frequent that he could see across the lake, but then the lake water began to swirl up into the air—something he had never seen before. The wind-driven water loudly pelted the side of the house, sounding like hail, and the windows seemed about to break.

John ran to join Mary. They stayed in the bathroom as the wind howled and their house shook. It sounded so bad that they did not know that the worst of the storm, the actual funnel, passed a few blocks south of them.

After the storm passed, the dawning light revealed wind-blown litter and some small trees down. There was not as much damage as John had imagined, as violent as the storm had sounded. The TV was still on. An announcer gravely reported an area where whole streets of houses had been demolished and, tragically, many people were dead. How many they were not sure, as all the missing had not yet been found. The area hit was only a few blocks away! John and Mary realized how easily they could have been among the casualties!

FIRE!

The next day, in another part of the country many miles from where John and Mary live, Ed and Nettie saw columns of smoke when they came home from church. They wondered aloud if the smoke was from burning brush or whether someone's house had caught fire. The smoke was not too close, though, so they did not feel threatened until, some hours later, they began to smell something acrid in the air. When they looked outside, the columns of smoke were much larger and much wider and the wind, stronger now, was blowing smoke in their direction.

Nettie turned on the TV and learned that the drought conditions had turned a campfire into a wildfire! The whole west side of their community was at risk. The weather advisory warned that residents might have to evacuate if the fire could not be put under control!

If they had to leave, what would they be able to take with them? Ed and Nettie thought of the irreplaceable items, their photographs and their most meaningful possessions—far too many to fit into the car.

Over the next two days, the smoke became heavier and it was becoming harder to breathe. Ash was falling like a light snow. With no rain in sight, the warnings were becoming more foreboding. Some of the neighbors already had begun to leave.

On the third day, Ed and Nettie reluctantly locked up their house and evacuated, having stayed a night longer than most of their neighbors. They drove about fifty miles away to stay with friends. Riveted to the TV coverage of the wildfire, their feeling of helplessness grew as the fire burned closer and finally began consuming the area where they lived. Aerial coverage showed house after house catching fire.

For several days after that, roads near their home were closed. Finally, Ed and Nettie could get through. The trees and brush on either side of the road home were charcoal black and stumps were smoldering when Ed and Nettie were still a few miles from where they had lived.

It was a strange, even eerie sight. Every so often something in what used to be roadside forest would ignite and fire would flash into the air, but since almost everything around the fire had already been burned, the flames would abruptly disappear. The smell of smoke hung heavily in the air and permeated the car. Radio reports told that hundreds of houses had been lost.

Finally they drove into what had been their neighborhood. Ed and Nettie felt disoriented. The familiar landmarks were gone. Here there was a house foundation covered with ash, there a partially destroyed house, then a few other foundations, then a house that looked almost untouched, then another that was only a shell! The neighborhood looked like something out of a war movie!

Suddenly it was no longer a movie. Ed and Nettie realized that the smoldering, ash-heaped foundation they were driving past had been . . . their home!

Gone! Everything!

FLOOD!

The Russell family huddled at the top of the stairs. The rain hadn't stopped for days and despite the community volunteers having sandbagged the river, the water broke through. When he heard about the flooding, Will Russell raced home, but by the time he arrived water was already swirling around the front steps. He sloshed into the house.

Margaret was inside with their three preschool children, trying to keep the children calm. Margaret and Will quickly and quietly, discussed what to do. Trying to take the small children through water (now knee-high for the parents but chest-high for the children) seemed like too much of a risk. Carrying the three children very far in their arms didn't seem possible, especially if the water level rose before they could reach their friend's house on higher ground. They decided to take everyone up the stairs to wait on the second floor. Surely the water couldn't rise that high!

At first it seemed like an adventure to the kids, but as the water inched up the stairwell, the anxiety that

Will and Margaret tried not to show eventually came through, and the children began to get louder and rowdier.

Just before reaching the top of the stairs, the water began to recede. "Thank God," Margaret said. Will just let out his breath with a sigh of relief.

A few hours later, the water was only about an inch high on the floor downstairs, but what a mess! Mud everywhere. The children slid back and forth, making all kinds of noise, falling down, stirring up the muddy water, becoming muddy themselves from head to toe. Will and Margaret could only shake their heads, not knowing where to start with the cleanup. Everything on the first floor that was not waterproof was lost! Pictures, stuffed toy animals, food in the pantry, everything! And the water was not only muddy but impure. From flooded septic tanks, the smell of raw sewage was in the air and in the house.

After as much cleanup as possible, the water stains on the walls seemed almost bearable until, day by day, the growing smell of mildew indicated that wallboard throughout the whole first floor would have to be removed—more mess and disruption!

EARTHQUAKE!

Lee had felt earth tremors before. Once on a business trip, in a hotel in the middle of the night, he had been awakened by an odd cracking sound in the walls. Then the large window and sliding glass door leading to the outdoor balcony began to rattle. Most alarming, he felt that the bed beneath him was on some kind of spring-like base that soon would bounce him off the bed onto the floor. Then the tremor stopped.

That was a couple of years ago. This time the tremor did not stop. Nor did it remain only a tremor. The walls cracked and the glass rattled like before, but then his whole apartment building began to shake. Lee ran outside as fast as he could to the most open space he could find. He lay down on the ground, not trusting his legs and balance to keep him upright. The sky above was clear blue and peaceful, but the earth below was heaving and rolling, looking like when a pet gets under a blanket and starts to move. Except this wasn't funny. He was feeling near panic.

When it was over, Lee wasn't sure it was over. Each tremor that followed lasted only for a short time, but Lee had no way of knowing whether the after-shock would stop or continue—and perhaps be an earthquake even stronger than before.

The damage to the neighborhood was incredible. What most amazed Lee was that, while there was extensive damage to his apartment building (one entire outside wall collapsed), the house to the south of his apartment building and the business to the north looked completely untouched. It was not until three buildings up the street that Lee saw another house that was almost completely demol-ished. Across the street, about six houses away, another house looked like it had been twisted and turned on its fractured foundation.

It was the most confusing sight Lee had ever seen, as if bombs had been placed under some of the dwellings and buildings, but randomly. Lee could not help thinking, "Why me, and not them? Why them, and not me?" Lee had no answers. He was too shaken.

HURRICANE!

"Maybe we should've left when we had the chance," Dick said. The bridge to the mainland was closed an hour ago. Now the only thing to do was to board up and buckle down. Joan glowered at Dick with a look that said "I told you so," barely keeping herself from saying the words out loud.

Later she would say the words. The palm trees out back near the pond were bent almost perpendicular to the ground. Branches and debris flew through the air. The usually placid pond was whipped by the wind into white caps. A contrast made sharper by the white caps, the water was murky and, if water could have feelings, the water looked angry.

The house creaked and crackled and the wind whistled through the screening around the pool. The pool screen puffed up in some places as if about to break loose from the supports. Night was falling and the wind was rising. The sounds were even scarier when you couldn't see what was making them.

Before the electricity failed, Dick and Joan saw on TV that the wind had been recorded coming in their direction at ninety-nine miles an hour and was predicted to become a Category 4 hurricane, which would be at least 131 miles per hour. If the house was making all this noise now, with the wind not yet ninety-nine, what would happen at 131?

All too soon they had their answer. Their neighbor's roof went first, half flying, half skimming across the pond. Then the inside of Dick and Joan's house began to expand and contract, as if the house were breathing in and out, just before the pressure released along with their roof, accompanied by the roaring rush of wind and rain.

Dick and Joan had no basement because the water table where they lived was so high. The safest location they had found was a storage place with a low ceiling near the air conditioning unit. They had retreated there when the droning of the wind changed to a whistling whine. Because the low ceiling was not attached to the roof, it held fast and Dick and Joan remained dry. Everything outside the storage place that was light enough was blown away by the wind. Everything, blown or not, was soaked by the rain.

The calm was a relief, but only until Dick and Joan remembered that if you are in the eye of the storm, after being beaten by the hurricane coming from one direction, you have to brace yourself to be beaten by the wind from the opposite direction! Would they be all right, and what would be left once the storm started up again? That's when Joan said it not just with her look, but out loud with real anger and fear: "Dick, I told you. . . ."

DISASTER:
AN ACT OF GOD?

What John and Mary, Ed and Nettie, the Russell family, and Lee, Dick, and Joan have in common is that they have experienced what some insurance policies call "an act of God."

This book is written for Christians and other persons of faith who have experienced a natural disaster and struggle to understand how the disaster could truly be "an act of God." It is also written for their family and friends, and for other helpers and caregivers who want to do their best to offer compassionate and caring help to those who are on the road to recovery from the disaster.

But first, let's be sure we have a common understanding of what a disaster is and why it raises the faith-questions it does.

WHEN IS A DISASTER A DISASTER?

Sometimes, when something bad happens to an individual or an individual family, it is thought of as a "disaster." Certainly, major crises in health, a tragic accident, serious vocational problems or loss of a job, school failure, marital or family breakups, or other significant disruptions in important relationships can produce a feeling of disaster and feel devastating to the individuals involved.

For people going through such crises, and for those who want to be of support to them, there are many books and other resources available to help deal with these challenging situations.

There are fewer resources for helping people through the kinds of disasters we discuss in this book—natural disasters where not just an individual or family but whole communities of individuals and families and congregations are overwhelmed. For example, the tornado that could have swept away John and Mary caused massive destruction in the community where they lived. Even worse, news reports the following morning announced that tornadoes had not only hit where John and Mary lived, but also cut a swath across much of the state, wiping out a number of neighborhoods and leaving behind many injured and dead.

Such a devastating disaster is far more than any congregation, community, or city can handle alone, and perhaps even more than a single state can handle alone. That's why some disasters are federally declared disasters.

When whole communities are overwhelmed by a disaster, resources must come from beyond. In addition to the state and the federal government, assistance is needed from helping organizations such as the Red Cross and the Salvation Army. Within the religious community, outside help comes not only from other congregations but also from affiliated groups such as denominational synods, dioceses, districts, conferences, or national religious bodies.

During any single year, there are thousands of lives affected by disastrous tornadoes, fires, floods, earthquakes, and hurricanes. This book is intended for those who experience such a disaster and for those who want to be of help to them.

FAITH-QUESTIONS

In contrast to disasters caused by human hands, such as tragic bombings or shocking school shootings, it is the natural disaster that is most likely to be referred to as an "act of God."

Most people have many questions after a devastating natural disaster. The questions are all the more poignant when there has been great loss of life and especially when children have been hurt or killed.

People of faith, who believe in God, have many of the same questions that others have after a disaster. In addition, the person of faith also has to come to terms with one of the most challenging of the faith-questions, whether the disaster is truly and literally an "act of God."

When we hear the words, "act of God," and think about those words, the implication seems to be that God is the source or cause of the disaster. Some even may offer their opinion as to exactly why God would send or cause the natural disaster. Some of those opinions may be that the disaster was sent as punishment for some sin or to teach a lesson.

It is understandable that Christians and others who believe in an all-powerful God would either think that a disaster is something God has actually caused to happen, literally an act of God, or be confused as to how such a disaster could happen.

Thinking of God as the cause of the disaster may affirm the almighty power of God but may also lead some believers to another question, that is, whether God is really a loving God. The reasoning seems to be that if God is almighty, then God has both the power to cause a disaster and the power to keep the disaster away. How could a loving God not keep the disaster from happening?

There are others who reason that if God is truly a loving God who would not cause such a disaster, then God must not be all-powerful or at least not powerful enough to keep the disaster from happening.

There are also those for whom the experience of a disaster so shakes their faith that they conclude that such a devastating event can only mean that there must be no God at all.

Few believers can experience a disaster and not have it raise at least some faith-questions. What are some of the questions that have occurred to you?

It is important that doubts and questions raised by a disaster be allowed to be expressed, because they are honest questions and honest doubts that, if not silenced, can lead to an even deeper faith.

Let's look more closely at the honest faith-question: "God, how could this terrible disaster happen—and especially to people of faith?"

The question about how bad things can happen to good people is not new. It is the theme of a popular and helpful book. It is also the question raised in the Bible by Job. The same question runs like a refrain through many of the psalms and the books of the prophets.

It is not an easy question. It is especially hard when children suffer or die in a disaster because, in the Bible, Jesus is shown as especially caring and protective of children.

Perhaps that is why Christians look for an answer to one who came to us as a child—Jesus.

Shortly after the birth of Jesus, there was the slaughter of the innocent children in Bethlehem—a disaster for those families, ordered by King Herod who feared the birth of "the king of the Jews" (Matt. 2:1-2). By killing all the children in and around Bethlehem two years old and under, Herod sought to secure his kingship.

After about thirty years, the Son of God once more was called the king of the Jews, when he was mocked and stripped and led away to be crucified, and on the inscription on the cross where Jesus was put to death (Matt. 27).

What is called the "theology of the cross" helps us to understand that the world's sin and evil and darkness is not caused by God, but into the darkness God chooses to come with light and life. "What has come into being in him was life, and the life was the light of all people. The light shines in the darkness and the darkness did not overcome it" (John 1:3b-5).

What the Bible tells us is that all that happens is not an act of God, but rather that, in all things that happen, God is active.

2

Act of God / Active God

Whether or not it fits your understanding of a disaster, there is something profound that we can learn if we are willing to say the words: an "act of God."

If you say out loud, an "act of God," and then say it again faster, and then faster, soon you will be proclaiming the promise that sustains those who go through a disaster, a promise that very much needs to be heard: an "active God!"

There are many ways in which Christians believe God is active in a time of disaster. Before we turn to those that come most easily to mind, let's consider three ways in which God is active that might not be as apparent.

GOD IS ACTIVE IN OUR QUESTIONS

Questions are not opposed to faith. Questions are one means by which faith seeks understanding.

Christians have many of the same questions that anyone else has during a time of disaster.

"Why?"

"What are we going to do?"

"Where do we go from here?"

Often, beneath the form of a question there is an additional question. For example, Will and Margaret Russell might ask, "How will we ever be able to clean up all of this mess?" Underneath that question, there may be the question: "Where can I get the strength to do what needs to be done?" Or underneath Ed and Nettie's question of "How could something like this happen?" may be the faith-question, "How could God let this happen to us?"

Sometimes family members and friends and helpers try to answer questions before they have fully understood what is being asked. Rarely will that help. In times of disaster, it is very important that honest questions be asked and that there be those who carefully listen to those questions, even when there is no apparent or immediate answer. For those Christians who have experienced a disaster, it is faithful to ask the honest questions of their heart.

For those who want to help Christians who have gone through a disaster, the crucial first step is to be sure to hear and understand the question that is being asked. For a caregiver to invite a person to clarify their heartfelt question is usually more helpful than prematurely trying to answer a question the caregiver may not have fully understood.

Honestly asking our questions is one way for God to be active during a disaster; it can bring the light of

Christ into the darkness of our situation. As we find ourselves asking deeper and deeper questions, we should not be surprised to find ourselves moving closer and closer to the questions raised by the cross of Christ. The light never shines so brightly as when it appears in utter darkness. There is no way to experience the joy of the resurrection except by way of the cross.

God is active in our questions as they lead us closer and closer to the cross of Christ.

> *If you are a Christian or a person of another faith who has experienced a natural disaster, what are the questions that you would like to ask God? Is there, as there was for Ed and Nettie, a question beneath your question? When we honestly ask our questions, God is active.*

GOD IS ACTIVE IN OUR CONFUSION

The biblical Greek word for "confusion" means instability, a state of disorder or disturbance. Disasters are times when stability is shaken, order has become disorder, and a prior tranquility is highly disturbed. Lee's experience with the earthquake was confusing as well as frightening.

How can God be active in our confusion? God is active as God was at the beginning of creation. The Genesis account is that "the earth was a formless void and darkness covered the face of the deep" when God said "Let there be light" (Gen. 1:2-3). It was out of chaos that order came. It is out of chaos that order continues to come.

Until we realize that any order that we create in our lives is not (and never can be) permanent, we have less reason to look for a higher order that can make sense of what is senseless to us. A disaster disorders us and requires that things be put back together in new ways. God is active in the midst of the reordering that is required after a disaster, helping us to reevaluate our priorities and to reconsider what comes first in our lives.

Confusion, like anger, is one of those feelings that often is accompanied by another feeling just under the surface. For example, underneath the feeling of confusion may be shock, surprise, hurt, disappointment, guilt, sadness, frustration, fear, or a number of other feelings. All the person may know is that they are feeling confused, but if the accompanying feelings are identified, then an important step has been taken in understanding what it is that is so confusing.

It is important for Christians to remember that to feel confused or to have other feelings is not unfaithful. What we do with our feelings, how we put a feeling into action, may be unfaithful, but having the feeling itself is not unfaithful.

If you are a Christian or a person of faith who has experienced a natural disaster, what are the feelings that you experienced during the disaster? As they did for John and Mary, did additional feelings arise during the days that immediately followed?

God is active in our lives when we acknowledge our feelings and let those feelings raise honest questions, even honest doubts.

GOD IS ACTIVE IN OUR DOUBTS

Having doubts can be disturbing to persons of faith, but God also is active in our doubts.

For those Christians born into and raised in the faith, as Dick was, there may have been few times in their lives when faith seemed to be a conscious choice. In the aftermath of a devastating disaster, doubts may arise and, along with those doubts, the necessity of choosing whether to believe that God is indeed active in the midst of all the mess.

There are other Christians, like Joan, for whom Christ was at one time in her life a very conscious choice. She found that going through the hurricane shook her earlier decision to trust in God. Even the disciples who left their former way of life to follow Jesus had to reconsider their discipleship when the "darkness came over the whole land" on the day of the crucifixion (Matt. 27:45).

The theology of the cross is a theology of choice. The first choice is God's. "You did not choose me but I chose you," Jesus said (John 15:16). That choice followed God's even earlier choice: "For God so loved the world that he gave his only son. . . ." (John 3:16).

After a disaster, Christians may have to deal with doubt that God so loves the world. It is honest and faithful to express doubts. God chose to come to us in Christ to lighten our darkness—which includes the darkness of doubt.

If you are a Christian or a person of another faith who has experienced a disaster, what doubts have been the most troublesome for you? With whom have you felt free to express your doubts?

One of the ways that God is active in our doubts is to invite us to see past the chaos, past the disorder, past the mess. When catastrophe strikes and all seems lost, faith is more clearly understood as "the assurance of things hoped for, the conviction of things not seen" (Hebrews 11:1). It is not only in times of disaster, but especially in times of disaster, that Christians are challenged to see with the eyes of faith.

3

Seeing with the Eyes of Faith

A spiritual way of seeing, seeing with the eyes of faith, is not something that we can do on our own. Such a spiritual way of seeing is a gift from God. It is one expression of the spirituality proclaimed by the apostle Paul:

> For this reason I bow my knees before the Father, from whom every family in heaven and on earth takes its name. I pray that, according to the riches of [God's] glory, [God] may grant that you may be strengthened in your inner being with power through [the] Spirit, and that Christ may dwell in your hearts through faith, as you are being rooted and grounded in love. I pray that you may have the power to comprehend, with all the saints, what is the breadth and length and height and depth, and to know the love of Christ that surpasses knowledge, so that you may be filled with all the fullness of God. (Ephesians 3:14-19)

On the basis of this passage from Ephesians, we can say that the eyes of faith see the cross of Christ at the center of life. "The spiritual is the height, length, breadth, and depth of the love of God that underlies, embraces, and transforms our personal and communal life together. Christians believe that God's love has been most clearly and gracefully revealed in Christ Jesus. Note that the symbol of the cross is created vertically (height and depth) and horizontally (length and breadth) (Harbaugh 1990, 100). Seeing with the eyes of faith is "a powerful, Christ-centered way of looking at life, the power of hopeful, positive, transformative "seeing," a power that is not our own but a gift from God (Harbaugh 2000, 148).

Through the eyes of faith, we see Christ present and caring for us in times of disaster, making it possible for us to "comprehend" with the heart if not with our mind. The word translated in Ephesians 3 as "comprehend" comes from a Greek word that can also mean "perceive." Especially when disaster darkens our vision, we pray that God will strengthen us in the inner person and give us power to perceive the presence and care of Christ.

With the eyes of faith, then, we look for what underlies what we see with ordinary eyes. With the eyes of faith we see the love that embraces us especially when we are hurting. With the eyes of faith we see the power of the Holy Spirit to enter into the disaster and transform our personal and communal darkness into light.

What we see through the eyes of faith underlying, embracing, and transforming our personal and communal life is God active in and through us, our near neighbors, and our faith community.

GOD IS ACTIVE IN AND THROUGH US

We have already seen that God is active in us as we honestly ask our questions. God also is active in us as we express our confusion and other feelings, and God is active in us as we acknowledge our doubts.

There is another way in which God is very personally active in us. Psalm 139 is in part a psalm of creation, the wonderful creation of the human person. With awe and wonder the psalmist praises the God who forms our inward parts and knits us together in our mothers' wombs.

In my book *God's Gifted People*, there is an exploration of some of the marvelous ways in which God knits us together and gifts us differently. While we may notice personality differences among people, we may not recognize that some of these differences in other people may actually be because they have received a differing personality gift from God. *God's Gifted People* looks at some of the different ways we take in information and come to a decision about the information we take in. In any group of people we also will find differences in how we connect and interact with the world, where our energy comes from, and how organized we prefer our life to be.

These differences among people can make a major difference in the way we experience a disaster and also in the way God can be active in us. For example, if Margaret is very much oriented to the outer world around her and takes in information through her senses (eyes, ears, nose, taste, and touch), the flood disaster would be devastating indeed. The water would cut her off from the outer world and the smell of sewage and mildew would totally assault her senses.

If Margaret is relationally oriented, she will characteristically take into careful consideration her most important relationships. She will not only be overwhelmed by what she has experienced but also be very concerned for what those most dear to her, her children and husband, have experienced. She will want any decisions she makes to keep in mind their needs as well. If Margaret prefers her personal world to be orderly, the disorder and messiness of a flood disaster would make it hard for her even to know where to begin to put things right. These same things would be true of any other person, female or male, who is outwardly and relationally oriented, who is keenly aware of sight and sound, and who prefers to live with order and organization.

But not all people are knit together by God in the special ways that Margaret is. Even though Lee, who experienced the earthquake, is like Margaret in relying on his senses, as a person oriented more to the inner world of thoughts and ideas than to the outer world, Lee may not feel the impact of the disaster as much in the external situation as in the internal disruption of his thoughts. If Lee highly values logic, the bewildering random destructiveness of the earthquake may assault his intellect as much as his senses.

Unlike Lee and Margaret, some persons do not have a sensory focus on what is actually or virtually in their face in the here and now. They may have been gifted by God in another way, equally wonderful but quite different. Rather than a focus on the here and now, some people more naturally look beyond the present moment to what will be possible in a few months. While it can be a helpful gift, to look beyond the present moment during a time of disaster, sometimes the hopefulness is short-lived. It is not unusual for what looks like a recovery period of only a few months to stretch into many months or even a few years. In reality, most people are unpleasantly surprised to learn how very long it takes to recover from a disaster.

Let's consider another common difference among people. Margaret's husband, Will, does not share her concern for order and organization and prefers a more flexible and adaptable life style. The disorganization of a disaster may be most disconcerting for those whose desire for orderliness has been disrupted. Even after the interior of a house has returned to some semblance of order, it is not unusual to wait many days for trash and debris to be picked up. For those who are like Margaret, having to look at constant reminders of the disorder can be much more troublesome than it might be for Will. On the other hand, flexibility has its limits, and even Will may find it challenging to make all of the adaptations that a catastrophe demands.

What these personal and personality differences suggest to us is that Margaret and Will, though married and living in the same house, may experience the same disaster in very different ways. And the individual ways in which Margaret and Will are affected by a disaster would not necessarily be the same ways that John, Mary, Ed, Nettie, Dick, Joan, the Russell children, and Lee are affected.

Individual differences in ways different persons experience a disaster also show up in additional ways. For example, two persons have had their houses badly damaged. For one, the sight of the structural damage is terribly hard to handle, along with the fear of not being able to make the rest of the house secure enough to stay there safely. For the other person whose house was equally badly damaged, the loss of the structure is far less traumatic than the loss of treasured memorabilia from a deceased relative, and other personal gifts that can never be replaced.

Other factors can affect an individual's response to a disaster. A person's state of health when a disaster strikes, their age, what is going on in their life at that time, the quality of their relationships, the supportiveness of family and friends, and many other personal variables affect how a disaster is experienced. These differences among people also may result in differences in the concerns and feelings that arise, and the long-term impact the disaster makes.

A person who has experienced a disaster can help those who want to help them. God is active in us as we help the helpers to understand what loss or stress is the greatest loss or stress that we are feeling. If we are willing to let those who want to be helpful know how the disaster has significantly impacted our life, this sharing can open the way for God to be active in supporting us through the ministry of others in ways that are more likely to feel truly supportive.

Given your personality and personal life circumstances, what has been the hardest part of the disaster to bear? What loss or stress has been most difficult? What would help most if someone were willing to offer it?

GOD IS ACTIVE IN AND THROUGH OUR NEIGHBOR

Disasters have a way of breaking down barriers that we may not have known existed. For instance, any of us could move into a community where there are fences between the houses. When we moved into the house with a fence around it, our intention may not have been to be cut off from our neighbor. The fence was already there. But, even though we may not have put the fence there, it may make it harder to meet and get to know our neighbor.

It was reported after one disastrous storm that winds had knocked down virtually all the existing fences. The report observed that people were becoming acquainted with their neighbors and helping each other, especially backyard neighbors they may previously never have met!

Seen with the eyes of faith, God did not blow down the fences, but God is active in the reaching out of neighbor to neighbor. In 1 John 4:11 we read: "Beloved, since God loved us so much, we also ought to love one another. . . . If we love one another, God lives in us, and his love is perfected in us." When a neighbor offers a helping hand, eyes of faith see not only the help but also the God who is helping us through the neighbor's kindness.

There are near neighbors and there are neighbors from the larger community who are willing to help in times of disaster. In a federally declared disaster, the Federal Emergency Management Agency (FEMA) and the Red Cross are on the scene as soon as possible. God works not only through the faith community but also through these community helpers.

Sometimes we look for God to act in only one way, perhaps through a pastor or a particular Christian friend, when God may actually already be responding to us in quite a different way than we expect. Christians who look with the eyes of faith see that God may choose to be active through any person or group, whether or not that person or group is a part of a faith community. In the Old Testament, God used a non-Jew to decree the rebuilding of the city and the temple in Jerusalem (Ezra 6, Nehemiah 2, Isaiah 44—45). All good gifts come from God and, during a time of disaster, God is active and works through many hands and hearts. In their presence and care, the eyes of faith see another way in which God is active in and through the neighbor.

But it is through the faith community that God's help is given most explicitly, and through the Christian faith community, help is given in the name of Jesus Christ.

GOD IS ACTIVE IN AND THROUGH OUR FAITH COMMUNITY

Now you are the body of Christ and individually members of it.
—1 Cor. 12:27

If one member suffers, all suffer together with it. . . .
—1 Cor. 12:26

A time of crisis has been described as both a danger and an opportunity. The dangers of a disaster are clear. The opportunities may not be. One of the greatest opportunities for the faith community in a time of disaster is to embody the love of God and the presence and care of Christ.

As members of the body of Christ, we are called by God to respond to the suffering of any part of the body. In response to that call, Church World Service and many denominations, such as the Presbyterian, Methodist, Disciples of Christ, United Church of

Christ, Mennonite, Brethren, and Lutheran churches, have special disaster response ministries. Sometimes denominational disaster responses are separate, with as much cooperation with other denominations as possible. In some geographical areas, and in particular disaster situations, the ecumenical and denominational disaster ministries may be joined together. The partnerships that work best in one situation may not in another. No two disasters are exactly alike. That means that no two disaster responses can be exactly alike.

Of course, there are some things the disaster response of any one denomination has in common with other denominational disaster responses. For that reason, many denominations will recognize themselves in parts of the following description of Lutheran Disaster Response.

Lutheran Disaster Response (LDR) is a cooperative ministry of the Evangelical Lutheran Church in America (ELCA) and the Lutheran Church—Missouri Synod (LCMS). It is supported by contributions to ELCA Domestic Disaster Response and LCMS World Relief. There is an emerging LDR Coalition, as LDR has increasingly been partnering with others, such as the expanding ministry of Camp Noah (originally established after ruinous floods in the upper Midwest), the Orphan Grain Train, Laborers for Christ, Mission Builders, LCMS World Relief, ELCA Domestic Disaster Response, Lutheran Hour Ministry, Aid Association for Lutherans, Lutheran Brotherhood, and Lutheran Services in America.

In anticipation of an imminent disaster such as an impending hurricane, or immediately after a major disaster, there is communication between LDR, representatives of the relevant denominational judicatory, and the closest Lutheran social service agency. If it appears that disaster response from the wider church may be helpful, plans are made for a needs assessment, usually as soon as there is access to the affected area. Judicatories, such as districts and synods, contact their ministers and congregations to assist with the needs assessment.

Once a disaster is seen to be of such proportion that the resources of the larger church are needed, Lutheran Disaster Response will characteristically make a commitment to continue the disaster response as long as the need continues. Federal, state, and community resources are very much needed and valued, but often their response in times of disaster is time-limited. For instance, great resources may pour in during the emergency phase of the disaster, and immediately thereafter, but after the first weeks or months the outside resources may begin to wind down their operations and eventually will leave.

Since it is not uncommon for recovery from a major disaster to take a year or even a number of years, the church knows the importance of being committed to be there for the entire duration of the disaster response. LDR and other denominational disaster responses understand themselves to be called to embody the love of an active God. The church's commitment is to continue embodying

God's promised presence as long as real need continues so God's people do not feel abandoned.

The assessment of how long the disaster-related needs continue is in part delegated by LDR to a local steering committee. Designated ministers of affected congregations are invited to become part of a steering committee, which includes LDR, a Lutheran social service agency, district and synod leaders, the ministers, and representatives of Aid Association for Lutherans and the Lutheran Brotherhood. There may be other steering committee partners, as appropriate.

Contributions from the wider church are administered by the steering committee on the basis of needs known to them as well as needs identified by ecumenical needs assessments and community "unmet needs" committees. While care is taken not to miss disaster-related needs of members of Lutheran congregations, help is given to any disaster-affected resident. Denominational affiliation, if any, is not a criterion for help. The criterion is disaster-related need.

Frequently, one or more members of the LDR steering committee is also active on a local ecumenical disaster response committee. Lutheran Disaster Response knows that, by definition, a major disaster creates needs greater than local resources can meet, and so ecumenical response is needed alongside denominational response. Needs that cannot be met effectively and faithfully by a denomination may be able to be met by a combination of denominational, ecumenical, and local community resources.

In addition to local efforts, LDR communicates with all other parts of the LCMS and the ELCA, advising them of the suffering being experienced by the disaster-affected part of the body of Christ. These communications identify the most pressing needs and the ways in which those outside the disaster area can be most supportive.

Along with financial and material contributions, LDR may also enlist volunteers to join in the recovery efforts. A staff to coordinate volunteer efforts is designated and new volunteers may arrive in the affected area to stay several weeks or more. Sometimes the living conditions for volunteers are very basic, as is understandable after a major disaster. Despite the hardships, the faith motivation of volunteers is so high that, in one recent hurricane disaster, over the period of one year, more than 650 volunteers rotated through the Lutheran Disaster Response, helping with more than 2,000 hurricane-damaged homes. The volunteers are in addition to staff who, along with a disaster coordinator, may include a volunteer coordinator, warehouse manager, construction coordinator, site coordinator, and others, depending on the situation and scope of the response.

Volunteers, staff members, ministers, and judicatory and agency staff all give themselves fully to the Lutheran Disaster Response, often in extraordinary ways for extended periods of time. Therefore, LDR has also established a "Care for the Caregiver" ministry. At appropriately helpful times, LDR gathers together groups of those who are making such remarkable efforts to help others in order to provide a time of care and support for these caregivers.

Participants in Care for the Caregiver gatherings are reminded that self-care for the sake of their ongoing ministry is a faithful way to nurture the gifts that God is giving through them. For caregivers to be able to maintain their ministry long-term, pacing is critically important. If volunteers and staff do not stop working before they become exhausted, it takes longer for them to regain their energy than if they had stopped for rest before they became totally depleted. Not all denominations have included this special focus, but Lutheran Disaster Response has learned that caregivers are better able to continue to provide the needed help when there is care for the caregiver.

There are denominational efforts other than Lutheran Disaster Response that offer very special ministries, sometimes with special emphases. For example, some denominations are well known for their remarkable commitment and ability to rebuild houses. Others have a reputation for outstanding case management. And interfaith efforts are able to expand certain ministries in community-wide efforts with financial, material, and other specialized resources that may not be readily available to an individual denomination. Since a disaster is so overwhelming, there is need both for the individual denominational response and also the partnered efforts of the faith community in embodying a loving and active God!

4

Seven Grace-full Blessings of an Active God

Grace is a gift—God's gift to us. Seen through the eyes of faith, a disaster calls us to a higher, deeper, and broader understanding of ourselves, our neighbors, and of God. The number seven appears in the Bible many times. Here are seven ways that seeing through the eyes of faith can transform a disaster into a time of grace-full blessing.

BY GOD'S GRACE, WE ARE MORE THAN WHAT WE HAVE OR WHAT WE DO

John and Mary were spared the full fury of the tornado that took many lives and destroyed many homes in their neighborhood. When they saw what had happened to so many others, and geographically so close to them, they were reminded that what we have and what we do can be gone in a moment.

In an achievement-oriented and materialistic society, personal worth is often based on what we accomplish and how many possessions we accumulate. If so, a disaster that wipes out our accomplishments and destroys what we possess can feel even more traumatic.

Since a disaster can take away in a few moments what we have worked for and acquired in a lifetime, through a disaster we can grow in our understanding that God's love is not conditional on worth as the world counts worth. God's love for us is not based on what we have or what we do, but on who we are as a child of God. We become a child of God not by way of our achievements but by the gift of God's love.

In our baptism, we are graced as a child of God, who calls us by name. We are precious to our God. Thus says the LORD, "I will not forget you. See, I have inscribed you on the palms of my hands"(Isa. 49:15-16). In a time of disaster when we can be separated from so much, it is truly good news that nothing can "separate us from the love of God in Christ Jesus" (Rom. 8:39).

BY GOD'S GRACE, A DISASTER
DOES NOT TEST US BEYOND
OUR ABILITY TO WITHSTAND

God is faithful, and (God) will not let you be
tested beyond your strength, but with the
testing (God) will also provide the way out
so that you may be able to endure it.
                              —1 Cor. 10:13

During a disaster and in the days immediately after-
ward, a disaster may feel overwhelming and beyond
our strength to cope with it. Imagine Ed and Nettie's thoughts when they drove into their fire-ravaged
community and almost drove past the charred and
smoking remains of what had been their home! By
definition, a disaster is beyond our ability to handle
it alone.

But we are not alone. The LORD is with us. And
the LORD is faithful. God promises that along with
any test that comes God will also provide a way to
endure it (1 Cor. 10:13). Paul is not saying that the
test comes from God; Paul says the "way out" comes
from God. Because God is faithful, we can count on
there being a way to endure.

BY GOD'S GRACE, WE CAN TAKE CHARGE
—OR WE CAN LET GO

In a "can-do" culture, we may mix up culture with
Christianity by thinking that to be faithful in a time of

disaster means to take charge and regain control as fast as possible. Significantly, it was not when the apostle Paul felt the strongest, but when he felt the weakest that he recognized his true strength in the LORD (2 Cor. 12:10).

In my book *The Confident Christian*, seeing with the eyes of faith is linked with "faith-hardiness." Faith-hardiness is defined as the ability to see "the challenges and the choices in times of change . . . confident that Christ is present and caring during those times" (Harbaugh 2000, 4). There are times when the challenge and the most faithful choice is to take charge of our situation. There are other times when the most faithful choice is to let go and let God speak to us through our weakness.

In a disaster situation, a great deal of stress is experienced if we try to take charge when what we really need to do is to let go. This may be helpful to keep in mind as we deal with one of the most unwelcome surprises for many who experience a disaster of any kind—how long it actually takes for full recovery.

The flood disaster that affected the Russell family also affected hundreds of other families. At first it seemed that it might take days, then weeks; then it became apparent that recovery would take months. In some disasters, it may take years! The reality is that it almost always takes longer than we think it will or should. After doing what realistically can be done to help the recovery process along, a more faithful approach may be to give up trying to control the date of full recovery and focus on how to live one day at a time. The confidence of the faith-hardy is that Christ cares and that the Lord will provide. "So do not worry about tomorrow. . . . Today's trouble is enough for today" (Matt. 6:34).

BY GOD'S GRACE, WE CAN BREATHE
IN AS WELL AS OUT

Related to taking charge when it is faithful to take charge, and letting go when it is more faithful to let go, is the faithfulness of pacing ourselves. We mentioned the critical importance of pacing earlier. Without understanding how long it takes for recovery from a disaster, sometimes those who have experienced a disaster (and sometimes the caregivers who are trying to help) go about trying to make the recovery go faster by charging full steam ahead—until they are completely exhausted.

When we make a non-stop dash toward recovery from a disaster, it's like breathing out and out and out and out—until one has to gasp for air! God can breathe out and out and out the breath of life, but we who are not the Creator were created to breathe in as well as out. Breathing in as well as out is faithful because it a way to acknowledge our finitude, our limitations, our need for God.

When we pace ourselves, faithfully accepting our dependence on God, we become more open to receiving help from those whom God sends to help us.

BY GOD'S GRACE, WE LEARN THE
BLESSING OF RECEIVING

Sometimes ministers speak of an "incarnational theology." The term may be unfamiliar. Put simply, God so loved us that God became incarnate, enfleshed, and came to us embodied in Christ Jesus. Through his self-giving death ("This is my body, which is given for you" Luke 22:19) and resurrection, God through the Holy Spirit sends us out as Christ's church, the body of Christ (Rom. 12; 1 Cor. 12) to use our differing gifts for the benefit and upbuilding of one another.

In order for God's gifts to others to be used for our benefit in a time of disaster, those of us who experience a disaster have to be willing to receive those gifts. That is not easy for everyone. Some people feel very uncomfortable asking for anything or receiving gifts from others.

The nature of the church, though, is not independence but interdependence. God created each part of the church (using the body as an example) to be dependent on the other parts. The hand needs the arm, the fingers need the hand, and all need the head, who is Christ.

One of the grace-full blessings that can come out of a disaster is that we realize even more fully how interdependent we are as God's people. We also can more fully appreciate how God uses the differing gifts of people to embody God's continuing love for us through Christ Jesus. The morning after the tornado, John contacted his pastor and, before the day was over, a church group of volunteers was providing food and shelter to some of those whose homes had been destroyed. To receive gifts from God that God sends through God's people is to do no less than to receive our Lord. Our willingness to receive in a time of need makes it possible for those whom God has called to use their gifts to help us to do what they have been called to do in the name of Jesus.

BY GOD'S GRACE, THROUGH A DISASTER WE LEARN HOW TO GIVE EVEN MORE FAITHFULLY

Those who have received the helping gifts of others during a time of disaster are often among the first to reach out to help others in their times of need. In that way, those who by God's grace have received are able to pass God's gifts along.

The experience of a disaster may make it possible to pass along even greater gifts than we have received. There are times when the well-meaning helper does not fully understand the kind of help that is most needed. In a house that is badly damaged, with part of the roof off, perhaps the helper is focused on the roof. The helper may not realize that a homeowner may be more immediately concerned about how to secure the rooms in the house that still have a roof so that the family can continue to live in the house safely while the larger and long-term repairs are made. In other words, some people learn by experiencing a disaster how important it is to start with what is most important to the person in need. Over and over again, helpers who learn to ask what would be most helpful are surprised to be told that what would be most helpful is something quite different than what they might have guessed. To put one single room in order may seem very little when there is significant damage to the house as a whole, but it can be exactly what feels most helpful to some people—a hopeful sign to them that order eventually will come out of the chaos.

There is another learning from being helped in a time of disaster that makes it possible to give even more helpfully to others. That learning is the importance of the balance between task and personal support. When the volunteers appeared at the Russell's door, at first it seemed like a gift from God. But when Margaret was upstairs with the children, and suddenly a volunteer came up the steps and startled her, she was torn between feeling helped and feeling trespassed upon. Sometimes a volunteer can let the damage to a house and the task of helping to fix it take precedence over the helper's sensitivity to the fact that the damaged house is still someone's home. Those who have experienced a disaster are more likely to know the value of balancing help with the task and sensitivity to the persons who are being helped.

A reminder: Not all who experience a disastrous loss are sensitive to the same things. If we have experienced the losses associated with a disaster, not everything that concerned us will concern someone else to the same extent. When those who have gone through a disaster reach out to others who are going through a disaster, if we are truly to help, we want to be careful to ask the one we seek to help what will help the most at this time. We also need to be prepared for the answer to that question to vary from day to day.

BY GOD'S GRACE, ALL THINGS CAN WORK TOGETHER FOR GOOD FOR THOSE WHO LOVE GOD

At the time of the disaster and for some time following, it is not always easy to see how all things will work together for good (Rom. 8:28). Only with the eyes of faith can we have the "assurance of things hoped for, the conviction of things not seen" (Heb. 11:1).

What we "see" depends on what we look at and how we look at it. It may be necessary to shift our frame of reference if we are to see with the eyes of faith the many ways in which God is active. Romans 12:2 suggests that transformation involves a renewing of our mind. When through transformation and the renewal of our mind we discern that God is actively working in all things for our good, we begin to see things differently.

There are many stories of persons of faith whose physical health was deteriorating, but who mentally, emotionally, and spiritually were getting stronger. When the apostle Paul had to contend with a thorn in the flesh, he did not focus on the thorn but on the grace of God in Christ Jesus, grace sufficient for him (2 Cor. 12:7-10). Seeing with the eyes of faith, perhaps some thorns can be perceived as splinters of the cross, reminding us that how we most faithfully bear a burden is not by our own strength but "with the strength that God supplies" (1 Peter 4:11). It is in our weakness, Paul says, that God's power is made perfect. A good that can come out of weakness is our greater awareness of the presence and power and provision of our gracious God.

Just so, the good that comes after a disaster may not be readily apparent if we only look at the destruction. Where God's promised good may show up is in the increased coping capacities, the greater resilience, the more faithful prioritizations, and the spiritual strengthening that comes from a greater reliance on God's love and the presence and power of the Holy Spirit.

Regardless of how well we cope with it, a disaster is a time of tremendous loss. When the personal and material losses are great, we sorrow. It is not only understandable, but also faithful to grieve our losses. The losses may not only be great, they may be multiple.

Sometimes a disaster strikes at times that are not the best in our lives. Perhaps we, or others we love, have been struggling with a serious health problem, or reeling from a marital or family disruption, or have significant financial problems, or have not yet dealt with a previous major loss. A disaster is disastrous even if it strikes when everything else is going well for us. If a disaster hits at a low point in our life, the loss is compounded and the combination can be even more devastating.

What makes it possible for us to grieve our losses but not be consumed by them? One of the passages used when Christians die is from 1 Thessalonians 4. Christians in biblical times, like Christians in all times, were sorrowful when a loved one died. These early Christians were not asked to stop grieving, but rather, as they grieved, to sorrow not as others who have no hope. It is hope that makes the difference. And since our hope is not in ourselves but in the presence and care of Christ, our hope does not fail. No matter how dark the shadowed valley, we are not alone. God is active, wanting to work in us and through us and around us for good.

In a disaster, will all things work together for good? Not necessarily. Can all things work for good? That is God's promise.

5

"Let Your Heart Take Courage!"

Wait for the LORD; be strong, and
let your heart take courage!
—PSALM 27:14

Those who have experienced a disaster and
would face the future with courage will find spiritual strengthening in worship, Bible study, and prayer.
These spiritual resources may seem pretty tradi-
tional, but the reality is that Christians for 2,000
years have found strength in these ways, and Christians continue to do so.

"O COME, LET US WORSHIP THE LORD"

Worship is an expression of our spirituality. We praise
and thank God. We hear God's word. We receive the
sacraments that name and nurture us. "In everything
by prayer and supplication with thanksgiving," we are

46

encouraged, "let your requests be made known to God. And the peace of God, which surpasses all understanding, will guard your hearts and your minds in Christ Jesus" (Phil. 4:6-7).

Those who have experienced a disaster often find themselves drawn to the worshiping community. Even when the church building itself has been damaged or destroyed, God's people find a way to come together for mutual consolation and strengthening and encouragement. Worship provides the nurturing food and drink of Word and Sacrament so very much needed for the journey to recovery.

Hymns and spiritual songs are part of worship and can be a special way to express thoughts and feelings. During a time of disaster, the words of certain hymns, combined with music, give rise to emotions that may not fully be known until the hymns are sung.

Some hymns have words and music composed specifically for a time of disaster, such as the meaningful words of the hymn "The Earth May Move: A Hymn of Hope" by Christine E. Iverson, set by her to a haunting melody:

> The earth may move, the fires burn;
>> the wind may blow, the waters rise
> But through it all, God is here.
> Winds blowing fiercely,
>> darkness completely encloses us.
> Yet God is here.

In the silence of the night,
    when all our hope has taken flight,
In a quiet voice, God speaks to us.
Deep in the midst of strife, calling us into life,
God breathes the dawn and hope is born.

When all the rain clouds will not stop
    and swollen rivers won't turn back,
When we have to leave the things we love,
When dreams are washed away
    with the surrounding clay,
The rock of God will not be moved.

In times like this when all we've made,
    the things we built, the plans we've laid
Seem to tumble down around our feet.
Just as a mother hen gathers chicks
    gently in under her wings,
So is God's love.

When tempers rage and riots burn,
    when reason fails and chaos rules,
When the spark of faith is growing dim,
Christ shines a burning light
    into the darkest night.
The lamp of life will not be hid.

Christ shines on through our tears,
    through our doubts and our fears,
God is here.

In addition to hymnody, there is an increasing number of other worship resources that have been gathered or designed especially for ministry following a disaster. Some denominational offices make these available for local congregational use. Preaching after a disaster can also be challenging. Most pastors have not been trained in seminary how to proclaim God's word most faithfully during a time of overwhelming community disaster. It would be helpful if denominations, in advance of a disaster, would provide guidance for any pastor who suddenly is faced with the responsibility and opportunity of proclamation in a disaster area. In the section that follows, some of the biblical passages that have been helpful during disaster recovery may be appropriate texts for proclamation as well as being meaningful passages for helpful Bible studies.

"ALL SCRIPTURE IS INSPIRED BY GOD"

All scripture is inspired by God and is useful
for teaching, for reproof, for correction, and
for training in righteousness, so that everyone
who belongs to God may be proficient,
equipped for every good work.
                        —2 Tim. 3:16-17

Both the Old and New Testament point us to the word of God as a resource for life and ministry. The Gospel of John is further known for using the word (lowercase w) to point us to the living Word (capital W) who became flesh and dwelled among us, "full of grace and truth. . . . The law indeed was given through Moses; grace and truth came through Jesus Christ" (John 1:14, 17).

During a time of disaster, there is no substitute for turning to the word of God. Throughout this book, we have lifted up passages from scripture that speak to us of hope and promise. Keep in mind that the biblical passages that speak to someone else may be different from those which speak most clearly and meaningfully to you.

Some of the biblical passages I find most helpful in a time of disaster have been identified earlier. Among the most helpful Bible verses for persons who have experienced a disaster, and for family, friends, and caregivers who minister to them, are the following:

Genesis 12, 15, and 17

Abram (Abraham) was called by God to go forth in faith, with confidence in God's covenant promises.

Exodus 3

Moses at the burning bush is empowered by the LORD to lead God's people out of a very bad situation. Moses wonders who he is to do this. God's answer: "I will be with you."

Deuteronomy 30:19

Every day of recovery from disaster requires choices. Decisions that are expressions of our faith in God are ways we "choose life."

1 Kings 19:11-13

A great wind, an earthquake, a fire, and sheer silence. Then the LORD speaks.

Ezra-Nehemiah

The Temple and the city of Jerusalem are rebuilt (see also Isaiah 44-45).

Job 38

The LORD answers Job out of the whirlwind.

Psalms of trust and hope
(partial list)

Psalm 3: "You, O LORD, are a shield around me."

4: "The LORD hears when I call."

11: "In the LORD I take refuge."

16: "I bless the LORD who gives me counsel. . . . he is at my right hand."

18: "The LORD is my rock, my fortress, and my deliverer." See also Psalm 73:23.

20: "I know that the LORD will help his anointed."

23: "Though I walk through the darkest valley, I fear no evil."

27: "The LORD is my light and my salvation; whom shall I fear? . . . Wait for the LORD; be strong, and let your heart take courage."

34: "The eyes of the LORD are on the righteous, and his ears are open to their cry."

43: "My help and my God. . . ."

61: "Refuge under the shelter of your wings. . . ."

62: "He alone is my rock . . . my fortress; I shall never be shaken."

71: "For you, O Lord, are my hope, my trust."

91: "I will deliver . . . I will protect . . . I will answer." "Shelter of the Most High."

105: "Seek the Lord and his strength."

116: "I love the Lord, because he has heard my voice and my supplications."

118: "His steadfast love endures forever."

121: "I will lift up my eyes to the hills . . . My help comes from the Lord."

139: "Your hand shall lead me, and your right hand shall hold me fast."

Psalms expressing the feelings and faith of those facing hard times (partial list)

Psalm 5: "Listen to my cry."

22: "My God, my God, why have you forsaken me?"

40: "O Lord, make haste to help me."

42: "I say to God, my rock, 'Why have you forgotten me?'"

57: "Be merciful to me, O God, be merciful to me. . . . in the shadow of your wings I will take refuge, until the destroying storms pass by."

77: "I cry aloud to God . . . that he may hear me."

102: "Do not hide your face from me in the day of my distress."

130: "Out of the depths I cry to you, O LORD. LORD, hear my voice!"

Psalms that glorify God as God
(partial list)

Psalm 8: "O LORD . . . how majestic is your name in all the earth!"

19: "The heavens are telling the glory of God."

24: "The earth is the LORD's and all that is in it."

29: "The voice of the LORD is over the waters."

67: "May God continue to bless us."

90: "LORD, you have been our dwelling place in all generations."

95: "For he is our God, and we are the people of his pasture."

96: "O sing to the LORD a new song."

97: "The LORD is king! Let the earth rejoice."

100: "Know that the LORD is God. It is he that made us, and we are his."

103: "Bless the LORD, O my soul, and all that is within me, bless his holy name."

104: "O LORD my God, you are very great . . . You renew the face of the ground."

148: "Praise the LORD from the heavens."

Other biblical passages of comfort and hope

Ecclesiastes 3
"A time to break down, and a time to build up. . . . A time to weep, and a time to laugh."

Isaiah 40
"Comfort, O comfort my people." "Eagles' wings."

Isaiah 44
"Do not fear, or be afraid . . . you will not be forgotten by me."

Isaiah 49
"For the LORD . . . will have compassion on his suffering ones."

"I will not forget you . . . I have inscribed you on the palms of my hands."

Jeremiah 31
"I have loved you with an everlasting love."

Lamentations 3
"The steadfast love of the LORD never ceases, his mercies never come to an end; they are new every morning; great is your faithfulness."

Ezekiel 34
"I will seek the lost, and I will bring back the strayed, and I will bind up the injured, and I will strengthen the weak. . . . "

Joel 3
"The LORD is a refuge for his people, a stronghold for the people of Israel."

Habakkuk 3
"I will exalt in the God of my salvation. God, the LORD, is my strength."

Matthew 6:29-34
"Do not worry about tomorrow. . . ." God's care in anxious times.

Mark 4:39-41
Jesus stills the storm.

Luke 11:1-13
Persistence in prayer.

John 3:16
The good news of God's love.

John 14:27
"Do not let your hearts be troubled."

Romans 5:3-5
Suffering leads to hope, assured by God's love.

Romans 6:1-11
The dynamic of death and resurrection.

Romans 8:31-39

Nothing can separate us from the love of God in Christ Jesus our LORD.

1 Corinthians 10:13

"God is faithful, and he will not let you be tested beyond your strength."

1 Corinthians 12:12-31

"If one member suffers, all suffer together." The body of Christ and our relationship with one another.

2 Corinthians 5:16-18

A new creation and the ministry of reconciliation.

2 Corinthians 12:7-10

God's power made perfect in our weakness. "My grace is sufficient for you."

Galatians 6:2

Bear one another's burdens.

Ephesians 4:1-15

Unity in faith, diversity in gifts.

Philippians 4:6-7

"The LORD is near. Do not worry about anything."

Philippians 4:13

"I can do all things through him who strengthens me."

Colossians 3:16-17

Do everything in the name of the LORD Jesus, giving thanks to God.

1 Thessalonians 4:13-18
Encouraging words when loved ones are lost.

Hebrews 11—12
The "assurance of things hoped for" and biblical examples of faith.

Hebrews 13:1-2
Hospitality to strangers.

James 1:22; 2:14-18
Hearing and doing the word.

1 Peter 1:3-9
Hope in time of suffering.

1 Peter 4:8-11
The spirit of faithful service.

1 John 3:18
Love "not in word or speech, but in truth and action."

Revelation 7 and 21
Christian hope.

"PRAY WITHOUT CEASING"

When sorely tested by a disaster, worship and Bible study are spiritual resources that God provides, fulfilling the promise that there will be a way for us to endure. Prayer is another spiritual resource that uplifts both those who have suffered a disaster, and those who seek to be supportive.

Whether informal and spontaneous or more formal, prayer in any form is communication. Through prayer, we thank God for past blessings and pray that we be given the eyes of faith to see past the present disaster to a future filled with possibilities. We let our requests be made known to God. We ask for what we need. We intercede on behalf of the needs of others.

There are those whose health or life circumstances are such that they are unable to volunteer to help with recovery from a disaster. There are also those who have little wealth or material goods to share. Prayer is one way even those who cannot help in other ways can be supportive during a time of disaster. How very much it means to persons of faith who are dealing with a disaster to know that there are fellow believers throughout the country, and throughout the world, who are daily lifting them up in prayer!

For those living or helping in the disaster area, facing the challenges each day brings, it is strengthening to stop long enough to catch our breath and take an extra moment to breathe in the Spirit in prayer.

For prayer to be communication with God, listening is as important as speaking. Speaking and then maintaining silence allows space for the Holy Spirit to intercede for us when words fail, and for the Lord to speak to us in what the King James Version calls "a still small voice." "Now there was a great wind, so strong that it was splitting mountains and breaking rocks in pieces before the LORD, but the LORD was not in the wind; and after the wind an earthquake, but the LORD was not in the earthquake; and after the earthquake a fire, but the LORD was not in the fire, and after the fire a sound of sheer silence. . . . Then there came a voice to him. . . ." (1 Kings 19:11-13).

> *In response to your prayers, what is God saying to you as you recover from the disaster? The passage from 1 Kings invites us to consider that, if we only listen for a dramatic word from God, we may not hear the quiet words that God speaks through a family member, a friend, a caregiver. The Bible encourages us by reminding us that God hears our prayers and cares.*

With confidence that God answers our prayers, I share a parting prayer with you. From one of the Christian traditions comes a prayer that seems to capture the heart-felt cry of the Christian during a disaster and in the difficult days that follow. It is a simple prayer, filled with the confidence of faith, prayed to an active God. For you who have experienced a disaster, and for you who are called to be of help to them, I pray:

> Lord God, you have called your servants
> To ventures of which we cannot see the ending,
> By paths as yet untrodden,
> Through perils unknown.
> Give us faith to go out with good courage,
> Not knowing where we go,
> But only that your hand is leading us
> And your love supporting us;
> Through Jesus Christ our Lord.
>
> Lutheran Book of Worship, p. 137.

6

Faithful Self-Care and Caregiving

What follows are suggestions for self-care and for effective and faithful caregiving. The ideas have been shared in various Caring for the Caregiver workshops over the past ten years. After each suggestion, there is a question or two that you may find helpful as you take care of yourself for the sake of ministry.

In the blank space after each question, you might jot down your response as a personal reminder and for your future reference. If recovery from the disaster is not yet complete, responding to these same questions again in a few weeks or months might be useful, as self-care issues and needs tend to change over time.

1. It is faithful to do the best you can, even if it is not enough. By definition, a disaster is overwhelming, and so no matter what any individual human being can do to help, it can never be enough.

Question: In what ways is "it can never be enough" frustrating to you? In what ways is "it can never be enough" a faithful, healthy, and empowering perspective to maintain?

2. Help yourself and others in this spirit: "with the strength that God supplies, so that God may be glorified in all things through Jesus Christ. To him belong the glory and the power forever and ever. Amen." (1 Peter 4:11)

Question: How does helping yourself and others in this spirit make a more faithful witness than if others were simply to see you as a strong individual?

3. Ministry is not only doing things yourself but also equipping other saints for the work of ministry (Eph. 4:12).

Question: How have you assisted another helper to be more effective and faithful both in caregiving and self-care? Who in the distant or recent past has contributed to your being more effective in caregiving? In self-care?

4. A person experiences disaster as a whole person: physically, mentally, emotionally, socially, and spiritually. Where a person is especially vulnerable, there may be the greatest challenge to recovery from the losses following a disaster. One way to show the interrelationship and interactivity of these dimensions is through the use of the following graphic:

A Biblical Model of Wholeness

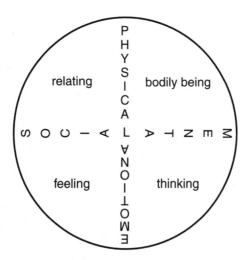

(W)holistic Model

Copyright © Gary L. Harbaugh

In this (w)holistic model, the use of the central letter L at the center shows that anything that significantly affects a person in one dimension, such as the physical, will also affect how that person thinks and emotionally feels and interpersonally relates. Biblically, the spiritual is not one dimension alongside the others but is rather at the center of life and embraces all of life. Therefore, the central letter L is used in a deeper, more profound way, since "El" is one of the biblical names for God. This suggests that, spiritually, anything that significantly impacts the physical, mental, emotional, or social dimensions of a person of faith also raises faith-questions.

Question: How can this model be useful to keep in mind when you provide care for others? In the ministry of self-care, some people practice good self-care in one or two of these dimensions but neglect some of the others. For each of these dimensions, what is the most helpful way that you take care of yourself? For your self-care to be better balanced, is it the physical, mental, emotional, or social dimension that most needs your additional attention? How have you been impacted by the disaster physically, mentally, emotionally, and interpersonally? In which area has the impact been greatest? What are the most challenging faith-questions that the disaster raised for you?

5. Every change and transition involves loss. Much of disaster ministry is grief ministry. It is faithful to acknowledge and grieve our losses. Granger Westberg's book, *Good Grief,* and other books on grief are helpful in identifying many of the feelings persons may have as they grieve a loss. Not all persons have all these feelings, but among the feelings that may accompany a major loss are shock, anxiety, panic, anger, resentment, guilt, depression, loneliness, helplessness, hopelessness, stress, and physical feelings of discomfort.

Question: In your care for others, which of these grief feelings have you most frequently seen? When you experience a loss yourself, which of these feelings are you most likely to experience? What other grief feelings are you aware of that might accompany a loss?

6. The losses caused by a disaster, for some, come soon after other major losses, such as the loss of a family member by death, the loss of a marriage, the loss of health, the loss of a job, etc. All of these losses may come together in the grief a person feels after a disaster. Moreover, since grief is a process, in which different feelings may come at different times, not all individuals, even in the same family, may be at the same point in the grief process. Caregiving is even more helpful when it is sensitive to these individual differences.

Question: In your own life, were there other significant losses that preceded the disaster? How has this affected your response to the disaster? To what would you want a caregiver to be especially sensitive, if that caregiver wanted to be most helpful to you? How can you use your own experience to be sensitive to the individuality of someone else's loss?

7. Some losses are very obvious, such as the destruction of a house. Because of personality and value differences, sometimes the losses significant to others are not as apparent. Even if a house has been spared, a gardening or aesthetically oriented homeowner may truly grieve the loss of a lawn, trees, shrubs, flowers, and beauty! Others losses are even less obvious but very hard for some individuals. For example, during a disaster we may lose our familiar patterns of living, lose a predictable schedule, lose our ability to get directly from "here" to "there," etc. While some of these losses are not as "great" as others, the accumulation of many small losses can be hard to bear.

Question: With your personality and values, what has been (or would be) the losses most difficult for you to experience in an overwhelming disaster? Which of the losses that are significant to you might be hard for helpers to know about without your telling them?

8. A disaster results in caregivers experiencing losses, too. There may be more losses than most caregivers realize. Disaster response meetings can take a lot of time. Preparing to help others takes time. Helping takes time. It is faithful to think: "This is really inconvenient. This is not what I planned. This is not fun." It is faithful to feel frustration and other feelings. It is faithful for caregivers to mourn their losses, even though their losses may be "small" in comparison to what some who have experienced the disaster have lost. Small does not mean insignificant. It frees caregivers to let themselves feel their own losses as they go out of their way to help others.

Question: In what ways has your daily life changed as a result of the disaster? When things change, something may be gained but other things may be lost. What losses have you experienced as a result of the changes due to the disaster?

9. As caregivers, how we go about helping others, our approach, and our spirit, may be as significant as the help we give. Caregivers have differing gifts, all of which are needed at different times in recovery from a disaster. Whatever the gifts we bring to recovery from disaster, Romans 12 invites us to use our gifts in good spirit, for example, "the giver, in generosity; the leader, in diligence; the compassionate, in cheerfulness."

Question: If someone were helping you during a recovery from a disaster, what approach to you would you most appreciate? How would the spirit of Romans 12 make it easier for a person to receive the help that is offered?

10. All disasters are different. There is also a difference between natural disasters and those disasters that result from human action or failure to act. While there are some things learned in one disaster situation that may apply to a following disaster, the specific questions and the feelings that arise in a time of disaster are in some ways always unique to the specific disaster situation. They are also in some ways unique to the specific persons who have experienced the disaster. The most helpful caregivers not only have learned from experience with previous disasters how to be supportive, but they also listen attentively so they do not miss and fail to respond to what is different, personal, or unique to the present disaster.

Question: What differences are there, in your opinion, between a natural disaster and a disaster that results from human action or failure to act? What is unique to the disaster you have experienced?

11. The Greeks had two words for time. There is *chronos* time, which is chronological time or clock time. There is also *kairos* time, a time of God's breaking into our life in ways that can transform our life situation. We cannot make a kairos time, but we want to do our best to remain open to the kairotic inbreaking of God.

Question: What signs are there that the recovery from the disaster may be a time of the kairotic inbreaking of God? What difference does it make if persons of faith look for those signs?

12. Why should one do disaster ministry? Christian disaster ministry is not best done out of a sense of duty or responsibility, but as the caregiver's response to God's gift of grace in Christ Jesus (John 3:16). Disaster response is one way for us to thank God for God's gift of Christ. Those who give out of a grateful heart are less likely to weary. We are also called to use our gifts in such a way that the Giver of all good gifts is seen through us. In that way, in all things God is glorified (1 Peter 4).

Question: What are the ways that you have found to give your gifts in disaster response so that God is seen as the source of your gifts? What words and actions seem to be most helpful in pointing to God as Giver?

13. The best preparation for helping others in a time of disaster is the deepening of our own spirituality. If our spirituality makes it possible for us to see in the midst of all the mess the love of God in Christ Jesus, then we will be able to make an even stronger witness to an active God.

Question: Worship, prayer, and Bible study are only some of the ways that persons of faith nurture their spirituality. What ways of nurturing your spirituality are most helpful in opening your eyes to see with the eyes of faith the presence and care of our Lord during this disaster?

14. Pastors and lay caregivers who have a prior relationship with the persons affected by a disaster may be all the better able to understand the impact of the disaster on the individual person or family. Ministry following a disaster can be all the more helpful when caregivers let their prior relationship with individuals and families help shape the disaster response.

Question: Sometimes caregivers do not know the persons they want to assist. In recovering from a disaster, what would be helpful for a caregiver to know about you so that their assistance would be as helpful as possible? How might a caregiver go about asking you for this information in a respectful way?

15. For a Christian, ministry is related to mission, and mission to ministry. A good question for Christian caregivers is how disaster ministry can be an expression of God's mission. Mission includes reaching out to others of different faiths, whether Christian or not, with God's love as an unconditional gift.

Question: What words or actions do you believe are most consistent with reaching out to others in a disaster as an expression of Christian mission while at the same time reaching out unconditionally, fully respecting an individual of another faith?

16. Disaster response ministry is a mutual ministry, with many actual and potential partners. Caregivers will be even more helpful to those they want to serve if they are open to communicating, networking, partnering, and cooperating with other helpers of good will and compassionate heart.

Question: What can denominational disaster responses offer that interfaith efforts cannot? What can interfaith disaster responses offer that denominational efforts cannot?

17. Self-care is crucial for caregivers who want to do disaster ministry over the long haul. One of the continuing concerns of caregivers is that self-care may feel selfish. It is not uncommon for caregivers to ask: "Should caregivers not be taking care of others without regard for care of self?" For those who feel guilty taking a little time to renew their energy and spirit, self-care may helpfully be understood as "self-care for the sake of ministry." In the days and weeks immediately after a disaster, if a caregiver waits to stop until there is no longer a need, there may never be a good time to stop. It is best to stop before exhaustion forces a stop, so recuperation does not take so long. By stepping back a little, a caregiver will usually be able to reenter the disaster response with all the more to give. Caregivers will also be able to continue in the disaster response for a longer period of time if they pace themselves.

Question: In what ways does it help to think of self-care as being for the sake of ministry? What other faithful reasons for self-care make it possible for you to pace yourself in disaster response? What can we learn from the gospel stories of Jesus about self-care and about self-care for the sake of ministry?

18. If the local and wider Christian church wearies and drops out before recovery from a disaster, those who look to the church for help may feel abandoned by the church. They may also feel abandoned by God. The church has a special concern that people not feel abandoned by God. Caregivers witness to a God who does not leave us comfortless and will continue to be present. Self-care that makes it possible for the faith community to sustain a long-term disaster response is faithful.

Question: How can the church witness most effectively to the Lord's presence during the first days of a disaster response? In what additional ways might this witness most helpfully be made as the days of disaster response turn to weeks and months or years? What self-care is needed for the sake of this longer term ministry?

19. We are not creators. We are creatures who want to help and care in the name of God, but we are not God. Breathing in as well as out and stopping before we have to are ways we acknowledge and accept our human limitations. This helps us look up for the true source of the strength we need for the journey.

Question: Sometimes it is faithful to take charge. Sometimes it is faithful to let go. How do you discern when God is calling on you to take control, and when God is calling on you to recognize human limitations and place things completely in God's hands?

20. We show our Christian love through active listening. Listening carefully before helping is the first step in real help. Caregivers may hear negative thoughts and feelings expressed about God. There is no need to speak in defense of God. "Being there" in the Name of God and listening to the frustration and anger and fear, while continuing to stand with and walk beside those who walk through the valley of the shadow of a disaster, embodies and communicates as clearly as anything we can say that Christ is truly present and caring.

Question: If there has ever been a time in your life when someone, by "being there," helped you to know that Christ was present and caring, what did that person do or say that helped you know the Lord was with you? In what ways does listening, even in the absence of words and other actions, help communicate the presence and care of Christ?

FINAL THOUGHTS

God bless you during this time of recovery from disaster. Remember the prayer that we shared at the end of chapter 5 about being on "ventures of which we cannot see the ending, by paths as yet untrodden, through perils unknown." As we walk the path of recovery from disaster, our confidence is in an active God who loves us and leads us.

If you personally experienced the disaster, may you experience the leading of God's hand and the support of God's love. If you are a caring family member, friend, or caregiver called to help in the recovery from a disaster, may you also experience the leading of God's hand and the support of God's love. Insofar as you can faithfully apply what is written in this book, may it become for you one of the ways that our active God gracefully guides and lovingly lifts and supports you, through Jesus Christ our Lord.

Bibliography

Hall, Douglas John. *Lighten Our Darkness: Toward an Indigenous Theology of the Cross.* Philadelphia: Westminster, 1976.

Harbaugh, Gary L. "Active God." *The Lutheran,* 1993.

———. "Bombs, Minefields and Type," *Bulletin of Psychological Type,* 1994.

———. *The Confident Christian.* Minneapolis: Augsburg, 2000.

———. *God's Gifted People.* Expanded edition. Minneapolis: Augsburg, 1990.

———. *Pastor as Person.* Minneapolis: Augsburg, 1985.

———. "Personality and the Perception of Loss," *Library of Congress,* 1984.

———. "Type and Counseling in Loss Situations," *Bulletin of Psychological Type,* 1990.

Iverson, Christine E. "The Earth May Move: A Hymn of Hope." © 1995. Used with permission.

Kushner, Harold S. *When Bad Things Happen to Good People.* New York: Avon, 1994.

McCurley, Foster R. and Alan G. Weitzman. *Making Sense out of Sorrow: A Journey of Faith.* Valley Forge, Pa.: Trinity Press International, 1995.

Merriam-Webster's Collegiate Dictionary, 10th ed., s.v. "act of God."

Myers, Isabel Briggs. *Introduction to Type.* Sixth ed. Revised by Linda K. Kirby and Katharine D. Myers. Palo Alto: Consulting Psychologists Press, 1998.

Myers, Isabel Briggs and Peter B. Myers, Contributor, *Gifts Differing: Understanding Personality Type.* Palo Alto: Consulting Psychologists Press, 1980, 1995.

Soelle, Dorothee. *Suffering.* Trans. E. R. Kalin. Philadelphia: Fortress Press, 1984.

Tagliaferre, Lewis, and Gary L. Harbaugh. *Recovery from Loss.* Gainesville, Fl.: Center for Applications of Psychological Type, 2001.

Westberg, Granger. *Good Grief.* Philadelphia: Fortress Press, 1986.

Resources

LUTHERAN DISASTER RESPONSE

The Rev. Dr. Gilbert Furst, Director, ELCA Domestic Disaster Response, 8765 West Higgins Road, Chicago, IL 60631.

Elaine Richter Bryant, Director, LCMS World Relief, 1333 South Kirkwood Road, St. Louis, MO 63122.

CHURCH WORLD SERVICE

Church World Service
    http://www.churchworldservice.org
provides a CWS hotline with current information on CWS disaster response.

OTHER INTERNET LINKS

Disaster News Network:
    http://www.disasternews.net/

Links to a faith community's disaster response may be available through that faith community's web-page or website. For example, Lutheran responses to disaster can be found on several websites, such as:

http://www.elca.org

http://www.lcms.org (then go to LCMS www destination, LCMS World Relief).

The Church World Service webpage

http://www.churchworldservice.org

also offers "Denominations," which makes possible an Internet connection with all the CWS member denominations. Also, typing the name of a denomination or faith community of interest to you in an Internet Search feature may provide an Internet link with a faith community that is not listed among the CWS Partners and Links.